Popcorn

Planets

Chris Oxlade

WAYLAND

Explore the world with **Popcorn** - your complete first non-fiction library.

Look out for more titles in the **Popcorn** range. All books have the same format of simple text and striking images. Text is carefully matched to the pictures to help readers to identify and understand key vocabulary.
www.waylandbooks.co.uk/popcorn

Published by Wayland in 2012
Reprinted in 2012

Wayland
Hachette Children's Books
338 Euston Road
London NW1 3BH

Wayland Australia
Level 17/207 Kent Street
Sydney NSW 2000

Editor: Julia Adams
Designer: Robert Walster
Picture researcher: Julia Adams

British Library Cataloguing in Publication Data
Oxlade, Chris.
    Planets. -- (Popcorn. In space)
    1. Planets--Juvenile literature.
    I. Title II. Series
    523.3-dc22
ISBN 978 0 7502 6967 4

Printed and bound in China
First published in 2009 by Wayland

Wayland is a division of Hachette Children's Books,
an Hachette UK Company
www.hachette.co.uk

Acknowledgements:
Andy Crawford: 22, 23; Alamy: Martin
Harvey 4, Suzanne Long 10, Mark Garlick
18; Lunar and Planetary Laboratory: OFC;
NASA/JPL: 2, 19; NASA/Goddard Space
Flight Centre: 5; Shutterstock: oorka 14;
Science Photo Library: David A.
Hardy/Futures 50 Years in Space 11,
JPL/NASA 20, Roger Harris 1, 21, The
International Astronomical Union/Martin
Kornmesser 6/7, NASA/Johns Hopkins
University Applied Physics
Laboratory/Carnegie Institution of
Washington 8, Mark Garlik 9, NASA 13, 15,
16, NASA/ESA/STSCI/ Hubble Heritage
Team 12;

Contents

Planet Earth

The Earth is the place where we live.
Its surface is made up of land and water.

Most of the Earth's surface is covered in seas and oceans.

The Earth is a planet. From space, it
looks like a giant ball. The shape of
the Earth is called a sphere.

The Earth is sometimes called the Blue Planet.
Why do you think this is?

The solar system

The Earth is part of a group of eight planets. All the planets in this group travel around the Sun.

Earth is the third planet from the Sun.

Jupiter

Earth

Mercury

Mars

Venus

Sun

The planets are each at a different distance from the Sun. Together, the Sun and the planets are called the solar system.

Uranus

Neptune

Saturn

Mercury

The closest planet to the Sun is called Mercury. It is also the smallest planet in the solar system.

The surface of Mercury is covered with craters.

The side of Mercury that faces the Sun is extremely hot. The other side is freezing cold.

When the Sun shines on Mercury, it is hot enough on the surface to melt metal!

Venus

The closest planet to Earth is called Venus.
You can sometimes see Venus in the morning
or evening sky.

Venus looks like a very bright star in the sky.

Venus

Venus is covered with thick clouds.
The clouds trap heat from the Sun.
This makes Venus the hottest planet
in the solar system.

The sky on Venus is yellow and cloudy.

Mars

The surface of Mars is covered with red rocks and dust. This is why Mars is also called the Red Planet.

The top and bottom of Mars are covered with ice.

12

Many spacecraft have visited Mars.
Some have landed on the surface
to explore.

The Mars Exploration Rover
landed on Mars in January 2004.

The rocks
on Mars are red
because they are
rusty. Do you
know what
rust is?

Jupiter

The solar system's largest planet is Jupiter. It is so big that all the other planets could fit inside it.

Jupiter makes the Earth look tiny.

Earth

Jupiter

Jupiter is made of gas and liquid.

It is covered with bands of cloud.

There are giant storms in the clouds.

This swirl of cloud is called the Great Red Spot.

Saturn

The giant planet Saturn is made of gas and liquid. Its surface is covered with bands of clouds.

This red mark is a thunderstorm on Saturn called the Red Dragon.

Saturn is famous for its rings.
The rings are made up of
millions of lumps of ice.

The black lines are the
gaps between
the rings.

Uranus

The surface of Uranus is very cold, because it is so far away from the Sun.

Uranus has some rings, but most of them are too dark to see.

The spacecraft Voyager 2 visited Uranus
in the year 1986. It took nine years to
travel from Earth to Uranus.

Voyager took pictures of Uranus and sent them back to Earth.

Neptune

Neptune is the coldest planet in the solar system. It is about the same size as Uranus. It has some swirling clouds and storms.

From space, the storms on Neptune look like white streaks.

Neptune is the furthest planet from the Sun. It is named after the Roman god of the sea, because it looks blue.

From Neptune, the Sun looks like a dot of light.

Neptune is the stormiest planet in the solar system.

Planets Mobile

Make a mobile of the eight planets
to hang up in your room!

Mercury:	2 cm	Jupiter:	28 cm
Venus:	5 cm	Saturn:	24 cm
Earth:	5 cm	Uranus:	10 cm
Mars:	3 cm	Neptune:	10 cm

You will need:

• white card
• ruler • scissors
• sticky tape
• paints • string
• hole punch

1. Draw eight circles. These
will be the planets Check the
list above to find out how
wide they need to be. You can
use different round objects
to trace around.

2. Cut out each circle. Write
the name of each planet
on the back with a pencil.

3. Paint each planet. Look at the
photographs in this book to find
out the right colours and
patterns for each of them.

4. Use the hole punch to make one hole in each planet.

5. Use a long piece of string to thread all your planets. Make sure they are in the right order.

6. Now you can hang your solar system up in your room!

To add the Sun to your mobile, you will need to add a circle that is 1.75 metres wide.

Glossary

crater a dish-shaped hole in the surface of a planet

gas a gas has no shape and can be invisible. Air is a mixture of gases

liquid a runny material that takes the shape of its container

metal a strong, hard material that is often shiny

planet a giant ball of rock or liquid in space

rust a red substance. Rust forms when the metal iron is left in water for a long time

spacecraft a machine that travels through space

Index